Deuteronomy 11: 13-16 NLT

13 "If you carefully obey the commands I am giving you today, and if you love the Lord your God and serve him with all your heart and soul, 14 then he will send the rains in their proper seasons—the early and late rains—so you can bring in your harvests of grain, new wine, and olive oil. 15 He will give you lush pastureland for your livestock, and you yourselves will have all you want to eat.

16 But be careful. Don't let your heart be deceived so that you turn away from the Lord and serve and worship other gods. 17 If you do, the Lord's anger will burn against you. He will shut up the sky and hold back the rain, and the ground will fail to produce its harvests. Then you will quickly die in that good land the Lord is giving you."

Taqiyyah,
Thanks for your support. I pray
this book is a blessing.

Be Blessed
LAKessa

GOD IS NOT ON A POINT SYSTEM

*Expecting Rewards for
Your Obedience to God*

&

30-day Devotional

LaNessa Jackson

God Is Not On a Point System

A Dream Realized Inc.
P.O. Box 332131
Nashville, TN 37203
www.a-dreamrealized.com

Printed in the United States of America
Editor: Angela Waderker
ISBN: 978-1-7321593-0-3

LANESSA JACKSON

GOD
IS NOT ON A
POINT SYSTEM

EXPECTING REWARDS FOR YOUR OBEDIENCE TO GOD

DEDICATION

I dedicate this book to God and His son Jesus Christ for speaking this word into my heart and giving me the courage to share it. I also dedicate it to all my fathers in heaven, my dad – Alphonzo Jackson, my grandfather – Willie Lee Doby, Coach Lawrence Cole, and my two grandmothers, Catherine Doby and Mary Lee Jackson. Special thanks to my mom, Willie Mae Dobin, for believing in me and pushing me. Lastly, I dedicate this book to all my friends and family that supported me on this journey and throughout my life.

THANK YOU

First and foremost, I would like to thank my Lord and Savior Jesus Christ for entrusting me with this assignment. This experience has truly been a blessing.

Monica, my beloved friend and writing partner who pushed me to birth this book. Your persistence commitment and guidance played a major part in this dream becoming a reality.

Friends and family, for your continued support and for periodically asking about the progress of the book. It is finally here!

My past relationships, if not for our experiences and time together, I would not have been in a place mentally to receive this blessing from God.

Lastly, I would like to thank the readers of this book. I pray this book will be a blessing to you.

LaNessa

CONTENTS

PREFACE

When you embark on a God-given responsibility, directive, or assignment, you have a desired outcome. You want to either fulfill the responsibility, follow the directive, or complete the assignment. That is your end game. It's rare to find a Christian who doesn't have the desire to meet those God-given obligations. The satisfaction and peace of being in God's will is the internal motivation for most believers who wholeheartedly embrace the mission. There are times when people obey God's directions regarding a responsibility, directive, or assignment because they want something in return from God. They have a promise, petition, or aspiration they desire to be manifested. In this book, I call them "motives." This book was written to help you identify your motives through deep soul searching honestly questioning why you obey God. While reading this book, seriously examine yourself, your motives, and your relationship with God. I pray this book will invoke an in-depth self-evaluation that will result in a transformational mindset with positive changes. My goal is for you to understand the "why" behind your actions for God.

INTRODUCTION

To this day, I am still unclear on why God chose me to write about this subject matter. Nevertheless, I will be obedient and complete the assignment placed upon my life. About ten years ago God softly spoke to me and said "LaNessa, I am not on a point system." In addition, He said, "LaNessa, you must also tell my people the same." At that moment, I made a major mindset change for the positive, but I was also instantly intimidated by my newly assigned responsibility.

At the time, I was in my late twenties, living my best life, so I thought, and doing all I could to avoid being obedient to the assignment God placed in my heart. I was a confident, successful young lady who'd finished college and landed a wonderful job at a great company. I'd reached the point where I was financially secure. I was sitting on top of the world in Peoria, IL, however, one thing was missing: a husband.

A spouse was one of my heart's top desires. I wanted to be someone's wife, especially because I thought it would complete my life. I had developed the mindset that if I'm being obedient to God's word, following Jesus Christ's teachings, and living the best Christian life I can live, why hasn't God given me the desires of my heart? His word states in Psalm 37:4 - "Delight yourself in the Lord, and He will give you the desires of your heart." The top desire of my heart was a husband. My reasoning was, I tithed every month, I attended church every Sunday, I sung in the choir, I served faithfully in ministry, I volunteered when needed, and I tried to be the best daughter, sister, friend, employee, and person I could be. So, I couldn't help but to ask God why He hadn't rewarded me with my ultimate desire, in return for my "good deeds."

When people would ask me questions like, why are you still single or why aren't you married yet, it would only serve to remind me of the fact that I hadn't received my ultimate desire. My first thought was always if I knew the answer, I would certainly tell you, but instead I would say, "I'm waiting on God to bless me." Continually being asked these questions always put me in a bad place mentally, because I couldn't understand why I had to be asked those questions.

I spent countless hours contemplating why I was still single. I was confused because I was obedient. Then God finally spoke to me and said, "LaNessa, I am not on a point system. You don't get rewarded for being obedient or doing the right thing. This isn't a situation where you do something for me and I do something for you. You

4

should be obedient to me because I'm God, I care for you, and I loved you first." At that point, I had to ask myself what was the secret motive or "why" behind my good deeds and obedience to God? What was my end game?

As we go about our daily lives, how often do we take time to examine why we do what we do? Think about it. Why do you go to work? Why do you adhere to the values and standards you've established for yourself? Why do you go to church? Why do you attend a particular church? Why do you follow certain routines? Understanding the "why" helps you to recognize the reasons behind your actions. In my profession, we use a methodology called The Five Whys to assist with determining the root cause of a problem. The fundamental theory of The Five Whys is to keep asking "why," up to five times, until you reach a conclusion. I work in the Information Technology industry and we encounter technical issues daily. The two questions we always ask are what happened and why did it happen? Often, we're able to quickly articulate what happened, but determining the root cause, the "why", is regularly a challenge. Thus, we keep asking why until we come to a possible conclusion. My objective for this book is that you engage in the same type of persistence with your journey and quest for obedience to God. We will examine topics to help you obtain a more authentic relationship with God.

At the end of this book, there is a 30-day self-reflection devotional to assist you on this pursuit of authenticity with God. The devotional is organized by chapters, and there are questions focused on key principles of the chapter. Complete the devotional in a method that works best for you. You can complete it five days after reading each chapter, or you can read all the chapters, then complete the 30-day self-reflection devotional. The purpose is for you to spend time with God meditating on the questions to assist you on your quest towards a more authentic relationship with God. All that I ask is that you be sincere in your responses, because that is the only way to change your actual mindset. I pray that this book will be a blessing to you.

CHAPTER ONE

THE SYSTEM

Love the Lord your God with all your heart and with all your soul and with all your mind and with all your strength. The second is this: Love your neighbor as yourself. There is no commandment greater than these. Mark 12:30-31 NLT

God is not on a point system.

Extra credit and bonus points are examples of rewards students receive in school for completing more than what's required from the instructor. In many cases, this could enhance a student's chances of attaining a higher grade on an assignment or in a course. The instructor provides the details of an assignment including the maximum number of points the assignment is worth, and if they're feeling generous, they could provide an option for extra credit or bonus points. Students in an instructor's class have the option to complete the additional work, but the motivation may differ. Why are they voluntarily agreeing to complete the additional work? The reason could either be because they want to increase their chances of getting:

1. A higher grade on the assignment, or
2. A better final grade at the end of the semester.

After the student decides to complete the extra credit assignment, they start the process of finishing the primary assignment, and afterwards they begin working on the additional task that will provide them extra points. Some students, motivated by the rewards of a higher grade, will put a large amount of focus on the successful completion of the extra credit assignment. Generally, the bonus point assignment is challenging. Since students are on a strict deadline of finishing both tasks, the bonus assignment would cause many learners to take precious time away from the most important part, the main assignment.

The primary assignment is where one's attention should be focused, because it reinforces the student's understanding of the subject or concept being taught. On the other hand, the extra credit task enhances the primary assignment, but if you don't understand the foundational principles being taught, then the effort spent on completing extra credit task might not be time well spent. This behavior could also be observed in our Christian lives. As Christians, there are times we tend to concentrate more on what could be **considered** "extra credit" tasks like giving an extra offering, excessive

While God has made
Promises to us... has also
set commandments/assignments

kindness towards others, participation on every church ministry, volunteering for all outreach opportunities, and other small disingenuous sacrifices, instead of focusing on the true assignment God gave His followers which is found in Mark 12:30-31, "Love the Lord your God with all your heart and with all your soul and with all your mind and with all your strength.' The second is this: 'Love your neighbor as yourself.' There is no commandment greater than these." Having a keen focus on loving God would help ensure we are aligned to the fundamental principles God has for His followers.

Many times, as Christians, we think everything we do for Christ should be deemed extra credit and we should be rewarded accordingly with our desires, when actually those actions are part of our primary assignment. Our actions shouldn't be motivated by the potential to receive your desired reward, but rather our actions should be performed wholeheartedly with love to glorify God. John 14:15 states, "If you love me, obey my commandments." Therefore, why do we obey God? In return for our obedience to His commandments, do we expect Him to simply bless us? This question of "why" prompted me to write this book because I started questioning the motives behind my obedience.

As mentioned in the introduction, I expected God to bless me with my wants simply because I was obeying His commandments. I would tithe and expect God to bless me with a husband. I would volunteer my time in ministry and expect God to bless me with a husband. I would minister to other people by facilitating Bible studies sessions and expect God to bless me with a husband. I came to the realization that my motives were not pure. I had an idol, in which I'll talk more about in Chapter 4, and it was the desire to be married. God spoke to me and helped me understand that I would not receive the reward I wanted for simply obeying His commandments. He knew that my motives were impure, and I played host to an idol I thought was secret. How many of you are playing host to a secret idol that is motivating your actions for God? In Jeremiah 17:10, God states, "But I, the Lord, search all hearts and examine secret motives. I give all people their due rewards, according to what their actions deserve." God knows our hearts and provides rewards accordingly. It is noted that many of us have good intentions and God has blessed you greatly because of the purity of your heart. This book is focused on us with secret motives.

Actions are rewarded by God according to the motives of the heart. Since my actions were not pure in nature, could this be the reason I hadn't received my desired reward? God only knows the answer. I will assume since He convicted me on my motives for my actions toward Him, I needed to change my mindset. God provided a reality check because I wanted my actions to be pure. I wanted my faith in God to prevail. Hebrews 11:6 states, "And it is impossible to please God without faith. Anyone who wants to come to him must believe that God exists and that he rewards those who sincerely seek him." The two key words in this scripture are faith and sincerity. When we are conducting actions, we must have faith and they must be performed sincerely. Other words for sincerely include genuinely, earnestly, authentically and honestly. All these words point back to the state in which our heart should be when we obey God's commandments, and *then* He will reward us.

We should not expect "bonus points" for our good work as Christians. Good work performed purely could result in favor from God, as mentioned in Psalm 5:12, "Surely, Lord, you bless the righteous; you surround them with your favor as with a shield." There are many scriptures in the Bible that highlight rewards for actions, but the prerequisite is you must be righteous and humble in your actions too. God is the creator of all things; therefore, He will provide your blessing in His own timing and according to the motives of your actions. We must understand this concept and ensure our motives are sincere. You cannot perform anything extra to get God to provide you the rewards He has in store for you. There are times when many of us have good intentions and we are still not rewarded with our desires. In those situations, God's timing and your timing might not be the same. Continue to do what God placed in your heart and He will reward in due season. So, why are you obedient? Is it for your glory, or His glory? What's your end game? **God is not on a point system.**

End game: I'd like to think it's to let all of me glorify christ by being the best servant I could be......

What started my desire to be obedient was my heart break/distress, peak point of Romantic Relationships (particularly Bryan) & my decision making — (eg. celibacy) men I like; I figured if I joined the fold started committing to God, heart break & "bad" decisions wouldn't continue w/ happen.... now I'm all in because I say I want God's will for me but deep down inside I'm hoping my obedience, commitment will get me things like:

- a job that not only allows me to serve but has power & money

✳ a marriage to show LOVE ▓▓ in a healthy manner

- to break generational cycles/curses
- clarity on purpose in life....

Although these are some of my deepest darkest motives that I say I want to "please" God.

I really want my motives/desires/my heart to be checked so that I may sincerely obey regardless of what's to come; no fear not

12

(right margin, vertical text) holding on curl of "might" get but holding because God said so & to lift up the King & His kingdom

CHAPTER TWO

GAMBLING WITH GOD'S GRACE

He will judge everyone according to what they have done. He will give eternal life to those who keep on doing good, seeking after the glory and honor and immortality that God offers. But he will pour out his anger and wrath on those who live for themselves, who refuse to obey the truth and instead live lives of wickedness. Romans 2:6-8 NLT

Gambling with God's grace can be dangerous.

God's amazing grace was given to us when we believed. We didn't have to perform any additional works to earn grace, it is a gift from God according to Ephesians 2:8. So if we can't do anything to earn God's grace, then what are our motives for being obedient to God? It couldn't be to receive His grace. If your motives for obeying are driven by the hope that you will get your secret desire in return, then you are gambling with God's grace. Why was the word gambling used? According to Dictonary.com, to gamble is to "take risky action

13

in the hope of a desired result." Having impure motives in your obedience, I believe, could be considered a risky action. God's grace is a precious gift to us, and even though we can't earn it, I believe we can pursue actions to have the need for His grace increase in our lives. Meaning, we are subconsciously influenced by our impure motives that God must continue to extend His grace to help us align to the path He has set for our lives. James 4:6 states: "But He gives us even more grace to stand against such evil desires." God wants His children to be humble, thus He might provide more grace in the form of unpleasant consequences to assist us on the path of humility and pureness.

If we have an underlying secret in our actions that is in direct opposition to the obedience of God, it could be viewed as using God. Yes, using God. Do you think it's fair that God's children are only obeying Him because they want something in return? In John 6:26–27, it states: "Jesus replied, "I tell you the truth, you want to be with me because I fed you, not because you understood the miraculous signs. But don't be so concerned about perishable things like food. Spend your energy seeking the eternal life that the Son of Man can give you. For God the Father has given me the seal of His approval." This scripture appears to emphasize the fact that people only followed Him because He performed a miracle by feeding them, but it appears they've missed the point of Jesus offering them eternal life. In your life, I am sure you don't appreciate being used, so don't you think God would feel the same way? The thought of the people He loved first, and saved, using Him for the gifts He can provide could be hurtful. To do His work repeatedly, not because they're glorifying Him, but because they secretly want something in return is deceptive. I'm sure God doesn't like to be taken advantage of, but this is where God's grace would multiply to refocus our motives towards pureness.

When gambling, the house *always* wins. The house always has an advantage because they make the rules. When you gamble with God's grace, and expect something in return for your obedience, God will *always* win. God is so merciful that He will alter the rules so you both will win. God wins when you complete your divine assignment and you win in receiving the many blessings He has promised. Please understand you may not win your desired reward, but you will win. Be thankful that God provided you with what *He* desired you to have because I guarantee His fortune will be better than anything you could have imagined. You will not leave God's house broke if you follow His rules. His rules are designed for you to win and in God's house, we are all winners.

Looking at the life of Jesus, His story is a perfect example of how God's winning is better than Jesus' desired winning. Jesus, on his way to the cross, prayed and asked God to remove this cup, meaning don't let what is ahead of Him (dying) come to pass. Jesus wanted to quit, but He knew He had to complete the assignment God outlined for Him. Matthew 26:39 states Jesus, "Going a little farther, he fell with his face to the ground and prayed, "My Father, if it is possible, may this cup be taken from me. Yet not as I will, but as you will." Since Jesus completed His true assignment, death for the sins of others, now Jesus has received the gift of enteral life, seated at the right hand of the Father. Jesus wanted His win to be not dying, but God provided Him the winning of everlasting life. I'll let you decide on whose winnings were better. Imagine how much better our lives could be if we played by God's rules and not cheated by having secret desires in relation to our obedience to God. Our lives could be fuller and happier because we aren't setting ourselves up for disappointment due to our expectations. We must trust that He will provide us with the desires of our heart. So, let us "delight ourselves in the Lord, and he will give us the desires of our heart." Psalm 37:4.

God provides rewards, but there is a minor stipulation. It is outlined in Hebrews 11:6, and it states that "he rewards those who sincerely seek him." Other translations use words like diligently or earnestly instead of sincerely. The base of the word sincerely is sincere, which is an adjective meaning 1) free of deceit, hypocrisy, or falseness; earnest: 2) genuine; real; pure; unmixed; unadulterated. Thus, God provides rewards when we are real and pure in our intentions to pursue Him and His plan for our lives. Starting today, let us be sincere with God in our actions for Him and the rewards will come. You know how you feel when you get rewarded for something you've done and you didn't expect anything in return? Doesn't it feel good? Let's have that same mindset with God. **Don't gamble with God's grace, he will *always* win.**

CHAPTER THREE

IT'S A SETUP

We destroy every proud obstacle that keeps people from knowing God. We capture their rebellious thoughts and teach them to obey Christ. 2 Corinthians 10:5 NLT

It's a setup by the enemy.

The enemy will use any trick to see God's plan defeated. The enemy will manufacture negative thoughts in your mind to get you to think you should be rewarded for your obedience. He's very clever and gets excited when he believes he has manipulated you, so he can try to obtain the upper hand on God. A great example is a familiar story we all know, Adam and Eve in the Garden of Eden. The devil convinces Eve that she and Adam will know the truth if they eat from the forbidden tree. They fell victim and succumbed to the desire of knowledge. He will do the same thing to you by tricking you into believing you deserve your desired reward because of your faithfulness to God.

One commonly used tick by the enemy is comparison. The devil will have you comparing your life to the lives of other brothers and sisters in Christ. You start paying attention to what others are doing. You see them going to church every Sunday, being a committed giver, holding various leadership positions and living honestly. You're doing the same things, the only difference is from your perspective, it appears they're being rewarded for their obedience. It appears you're always hearing about how God has acted in their lives and provided a miracle or their deepest desires. Their lives appear good. You see their blessings, but what you don't realize is the difference might be the fact that they have solidified their relationship with God. They have given all their desires over to God and they're obeying God for who He is and not solely for what He can do for them. What you might be observing are the rewards for their diligence and delight in Him. Deep in their hearts, they expect nothing from God for doing what He commanded and now they're receiving the blessings from His promises. The devil will make you covet others' rewards. Don't fall for this trick! Your God will reward you, but you must operate your commitment to God with a pure heart. We must combat the devil's seed of comparison which produces envy in our hearts. You are an overcomer.

Another tactic used by the enemy is distraction. The devil will trick you into thinking you are going down the right path, only to discover that isn't the path God desired for you. The trick with distraction is when you're finally starting to receive the deep desires of your heart, you find out the manifestation was superficial. Now, you're upset with God because your desires have faded away. You're questioning God, asking Him why me? You start reminding Him of all the things you've done for Him, but you don't realize that once you started to receive your desires, subconsciously, you started falling short on your commitments to Christ. This is where you fall into the trap of the devil, you are now distracted by the perceived gifts and you start to lose focus on your assignment. Once you discover you've been distracted, you feel like you've taken many steps backwards. This is distraction, and this is one of many tactics the enemy uses to get you off track.

The enemy maliciously preys on us by exploiting our desires, having us look at "The Joneses," highlighting the fact that we don't have what we've always wanted, then having us asking God why. Next, he feeds on our strong desire for our reward, and would have us disappointed with ourselves and God because we don't get what we want. Don't succumb to the enemy's tactics. You're smarter and stronger than that. Don't let the devil inject the wrong thinking in your mind, that you should be rewarded for your obedience. You know how the enemy operates, be prepared to defend yourself against him. In Ephesians 6:11-13, it says to "Put on the full armor of

God, so that you can take your stand against the devil's schemes. For our struggle is not against flesh and blood, but against the rulers, against the authorities, against the powers of this dark world, and against the spiritual forces of evil in the heavenly realms. Therefore, put on the full armor of God, so that when the day of the evil comes, you may be able to stand your ground, and after you have done everything, to stand." Each day, we must deny ourselves and be mindful that the evil one is at constant war, trying to obtain victory by wanting us to fall victim to our fleshly desires. God has provided us with everything we need to prevail against the enemy. When you have a subtle feeling in your heart convincing you that you should be rewarded for your obedience, when you know it's a part of your commitment as a follower of Jesus Christ, rebuke the devil. James 4:7 states, "So humble yourselves before God. Resist the devil, and he will flee from you." Take a stand against the enemy's maneuvers, which will try to distract you from prevailing in your true assignment.

Don't underestimate the works of the enemy. You have the power to outsmart the enemy by staying focused on God. You must be watchful. Tell yourself, I will be pure in my obedience to God. I am not going to move forward by doing God's assignments with secret motives in my heart and expecting rewards. The only thing I will expect is for God to keep his promises. Declare today that, you're going to obey God purely and wholeheartedly. The devil wants you to continue a life of being artificial with yourself and God. Destroy everything that keeps you from the rewards God has for you. When our motives are pure God will do the rest. He will reward those whom he deems ready to receive the reward. **Remember, it's a setup!**

CHAPTER FOUR

YOUR HEART IDOLS

The human heart is the most deceitful of all things, and desperately wicked. Who really knows how bad it is? Jeremiah 17:9 NLT

Your heart is deceitful.

Jeremiah 17:9 is very direct and honest on the position of our hearts. It will convince you to do what it thinks is the right thing or the thing that provides you satisfaction, even if it's wrong. Ever heard of something called the "flesh?" It plays a big role in convincing your heart to do things with the wrong intentions. Therefore, we all need to examine why we do what we do for Christ. Do we do it for personal gain? Do we do it expecting something in return? Or do we do it because we're obeying God?

Before we go any further, let's talk about "it." Your it could be giving, volunteering, reading your Bible, praying, or anything God petitions us to do. My "it" was giving. I thought if I gave regularly, I would eventually be blessed with my desire for a husband. My flesh led my heart's motive in a deceitful direction. My mindset was, I will give God my tithe every paycheck, so He can ultimately give me what I wanted. Thus, every time I received a paycheck, I gave faithfully because this might be the month I meet my husband. In addition, I would cheat God in my giving: I would tithe on my net pay instead of my gross pay. Side note: there were two things that finally convicted me, and I changed my giving pattern. First was my former pastor, Pastor Deveraux Hubbard. He was preaching a sermon on giving and he asked us if when we complete a loan application, did we list our gross or net income? When I thought about it, I would document my gross. Then shortly after that, I was also convicted when I was asked to lead a six-week Bible Study on giving. I thought to myself, how am I going to talk to God's people about tithing and I am not fully tithing myself? I examined my heart and started tithing on my gross. Please note, these convictions didn't influence my motives for giving. I still wanted a husband; thus, I had more soul searching to uncover the "why" do I tithe? I needed to search my heart.

The result of my soul searching was I realized that my heart was deceived. My "it" had become an idol. I idolized being married, so I secretly performed my obedience, tithing, to God because deep down I thought this would help me get what I wanted. My definition of an idol is, something you covet so seriously that it makes you lose focus on God's purpose. It could also be something you desire so deeply that you feel you can't live without it, or something where all your happiness lies. What are the idols in your heart? Psalm 106:36 states, "They worshiped their idols, which led to their downfall." When you don't have the right motives, you're worshipping your idols. Identify your idols quickly and give them to God to protect your future. You don't want it to be an agent of your downfall. There are times you may be blessed with what you want, but it could also be the thing that takes you out and the tough part is you didn't see the downfall coming. As you move forward, check the motives of your heart, course correct if needed, and let God provide the rewards in His own way. Your blessings will be greater, and your chance of a major downfall will be decreased. The desire of our hearts should be to stay purely obedient in everything we do for Christ.

In your obedience, you could also be cheating God. What I mean is, you could be partially executing God's commandments just to say you're doing it, but not really executing them to your fullest potential. Earlier in the chapter, I mentioned I was a tither, but I was half doing it by tithing my net instead of my gross. I was being obedient, but I wasn't fully committed to tithing. Once I got my thought process in line with God, I've been blessed with more than I could've ever imagined. I believe the same thing can happen to you. Romans 2:11 says, "For God does not show favoritism." What areas in your Christian journey have you not fully committed to God? For you, it might not be tithing, it might be your time. Are you only giving Him time on Sunday, and not spending any time with Him during the week? It might be your talents. Are you using your talents to build God's kingdom? Whatever your area is, I pray you understand where you might be cheating God. Once you identify them, then commit your heart to be fully committed to God.

We as Christians need to challenge ourselves and continually examine our hearts against Jeremiah 17:9 to remind us that our hearts are deceitful and wicked. Our hearts, if not denied daily, could lead us down the wrong path. Do you know how bad your heart could be? As you embark on a new task or journey with God, always be honest with yourself regarding your intentions and motivations. We must consciously take steps to keep our hearts pure. Deeply examine every action taken. Once we take the right steps, God is so merciful and will continue to provide His covering for our actions because He knows we can't do it by ourselves. **Our hearts are deceitful.**

CHAPTER FIVE

RAISING YOUR MATURITY

So you must live as God's obedient children. Don't slip back into your old ways of living to satisfy your own desires. You didn't know any better then. 15 But now you must be holy in everything you do, just as God who chose you is holy. 1 Peter 1:14-15 NLT

We must excel to greater levels of maturity.

As children of God, our thinking must transcend to mature levels by understanding God is perfect and what He has planned for you will manifest in His timing. No amount of work on your part will speed up God's plan for you; His plan will prevail. You should focus on being consumed with trusting God, and He will as stated in Philippians 4:19, "... meet all your needs according to the riches of his glory in Christ Jesus." Take a moment and focus on previous experiences in your life where God has blessed you, especially when you didn't expect anything in return or you felt as if you didn't deserve His favor. Release any strongholds that are preventing you from being real with God. You have the power of the Holy Spirit to assist you in the process. My dear brothers and sisters obey God's commandments and expect nothing but his perfect provision. Allow Christ to guide you to all the wonderful blessings God has in store for His children. Develop a heart of gratitude. Moving to an attitude of thankfulness will overshadow the desires of secret expectations, because your thoughts will be focused on the blessings and not what you don't have. Expressing gratitude matures us to a point where we are happy that God loves us and are grateful for the opportunities provided to us by sending His Son to die for all of us. Being thankful will move you from a transactional relationship, where God is like a vending machine in which you deposit money and expect something in return, to an authentic relationship where you expect nothing from God, but His love.

God's love is wonderful. The great thing about it is, it's unconditional. It's a covering that will be with you in your innocent moments and convict you in your guilty ones. His love knows no boundaries. It is faithful, forgiving, fearless, hopeful, everlasting, authentic, and every positive affirmation you can conceive. God loved us first. God loves the genuine version of you as well as the corrupt version. Romans 5:8 states, "but God showed his great love for us by sending Christ to die for us while we were still sinners." God was so gracious and allowed His Son to die for you and me. When times get tough, you must hold on to God's plan for you and use it as the fuel in to drive your obedience. When you reach moments when you feel like God has forgotten you and your deepest desires, just remember His love for you and know God will provide your desires in His timing. God's love is something you don't have to search hard for because it is always there, especially in the moments when you don't think it is there. Understanding God's love will increase your maturity.

Completely trusting God will help move you a place where you stop worrying about your future. It allows you to move to the mindset that God will provide what you need, when you need it. And if He grants you your desires as well, even better. Trusting God fully takes the mental pressure off you and places it on Him providing you an opportunity for an anxiety free life. Oh, how great would a worry-free life be? Philippians 4:6-7, is a great outline on worry-free living, "Don't worry about anything; instead, pray about everything. Tell God what you need and thank Him for all he has done. Then you will experience God's peace, which exceeds anything we can understand. His peace will guard your heart and mind as you live in Christ Jesus." Confidently believe God can handle all your desires. All He asks is for you to trust Him and He will provide your desires in His perfect timing. The only requirement of you is to trust, which is easier said than done. One reason this can be hard is because many of us like to be in control. Having the ability to dictate how and when something should happen is the only way some people can operate. Many believe if they are in control, then everything desired will happen at the right time based on their outlined plan. For example, I don't function well in chaos, so being in control helps me understand the big picture and puts me in my comfort zone. Thus, for me I need to deny myself daily. Matthew 16:24 states, "If any of you wants to be my follower, you must turn from your selfish ways, take up your cross, and follow me." Beloved you must give up control back to God, deny yourself daily and He will allow the perfect plan to manifest at the right time. This will increase your maturity. Another reason why it is difficult for us to trust is it can make you feel hopeless. Having unwavering faith is hard when there is no obvious path to get what is desired. Also, many may believe they don't deserve their desires based on their past. This is where maturity steps in. God is faithful and forgiving. When you feel hopeless, reaffirm your faith in God and know that His grace is all you need. 2 Corinthians 12:9 states, "But he said to me, My grace is sufficient for you, for my power is made perfect in weakness..." God's grace will cover you and His power, the same power that raised Jesus from the dead, will strengthen you as you navigate this season of hopelessness. Make a declaration today that you will put your total trust in God, obey his word, and don't expect anything in return but His love.

Maturity comes when you obey his word with pure intentions. When you sow into God's kingdom, sow because you desire to and nothing more. When you don't expect anything is when God will provide his greatest blessings. Sow your seed eagerly and God will bless you more than you can ask or think according to Ephesians 3:20. Let's transition to a level where we are experiencing the full blessings of God. Imagine how much lighter you'll feel once you stop worrying about the manifestation of your desires. Start believing if God wants you to have your desires He will make them come to pass when He is ready. Affirming that will take pressure off you and allow you freedom in your obedience. Romans 8:25 says, "but if we hope for what we see not, then we will wait for it with patience." Be hopeful in God. Trust he will keep his promise to you. Ask God to clean your heart of anything impure. Mature your actions accordingly. Our God is sovereign. **Declare today you will excel in your maturity in Him.**

CHAPTER SIX

SINCERELY OBEY GOD

Be careful to obey all these commands I am giving you. Show love to the Lord your God by walking in his ways and holding tightly to him. Deuteronomy 11:22 NLT

Sincere obedience fosters authentic worship.

I want to circle back to where we started, God is not on a point system. Understanding the motives behind your actions will help you to be truthful with yourself and God, which will also help you move towards sincere obedience. Sincere obedience will help you live a God focused life without the pressures of this world because you know God will keep his promise to all those who are pure in actions. In Matthew 5:8, one of the beatitudes states, "Blessed are the pure in heart for they should see God." Everyone should desire to see God in every area of their lives and he will be seen in all areas of genuine obedience. God is wonderful. He knows your desires and needs. Just give them over to His control and He will provide everything that's aligned to His will for your life. Operate in pureness. Ask God to search your heart and reveal the areas where you are not operating in pureness and once He reveals them to you, be open to acknowledging them and make a commitment to progress forward, in all areas, in pureness.

God put us on earth for a divine purpose. One of the great pleasures in life is to know you are operating in God's will. When you live in God's purpose you will experience freedom from many of the world's problems. Who wouldn't want a life of freedom, free from worry, disappointment and despair? As you search your heart while operating in God's divine purpose, work hard at focusing on only expecting the reward of God's love. Progression from childish behaviors, such as expecting rewards for doing the right thing, will help align you with God's purpose. Apostle Paul states in 1 Corinthians 13:11, "when I was a child, I spoke and thought and reasoned as a child. But when I grew up, I put away childish things." God desires you to behave as an adult, so you can be mature enough to receive the perfect will He has determined for your life.

Understanding all the topics discussed in this book will help us live a life of freedom and obedience. Chapter One talked about focusing on your true assignment and understanding the motives for obeying God. Our actions shouldn't be motivated by the potential of receiving our desired reward, but we should perform all actions with sincerity and purity and God will provide the rewards accordingly. Don't expect rewards for your obedience. Chapter Two discussed how gambling with God's grace with impure motives is a risky bet because God will always win. God's grace is freely given to the humble and playing by God's rules will yield great blessings. Decide to play by God's rules. Chapter Three highlighted how the enemy will try to use you to try and defeat God's plan by manufacturing negative thoughts on how you should be rewarded for your obedience. Always be on alert for the enemy's attack, you are stronger and smarter because you have God on your side. Keep a watchful eye. In Chapter Four, we talked about the deceitfulness of the heart and how we must constantly examine our heart for idols. Identify your idols and give them to God to protect your future. Chapter Five challenged us to elevate our thinking to know for every situation God has a perfect plan for you and it will prevail. Have a mindset of gratitude and expect nothing from God, but His love. Rest assured God will perform everything in his own timing. Lastly, in this Chapter, we emphasized how operating in sincere obedience will foster authentic worship and ensure the pressures of our desires will not consume you.

God knows your every thought, including your motives. As written in Jeremiah 17:10, "the lord searches all hearts and examine secret motives." Operate in obedience as you go about your daily life, including examining your motives and removing any corrupt intentions. If you find any misaligned motives, ask yourself why and give them over to God for removal. God will reward sincerity. Give your desires to God, He can handle them. Make a commitment that your obedience will have no secret motives and you will obey Him because you love Him. Let love be the guidepost in everything you do. **Sincere obedience will conquer secret motives.**

GOD IS NOT ON A POINT SYSTEM

30-DAY
DEVOTIONAL

This 30-day devotional was designed to aid in deepening your relationship with God by providing an opportunity for focused self-evaluation. My hope is it will provide you with an understanding of why you obey God, and help you refocus the motives behind your obedience.

Please embark on this 30-day journey. My only request is for you to be authentic with yourself and God. I pray this 30-day devotional will be a blessing to you.

CHAPTER ONE

THE SYSTEM

DEVOTIONAL

CHAPTER ONE

THE SYSTEM

DAY ONE

Focus Verse: *But I, the Lord, search all hearts and examine secret motives. I give all people their due rewards, according to what their actions deserve.   Jeremiah 17:10 NLT*

Devotional Question: Think about a time when you were in school and your instructor provided you with an extra credit assignment, what was your motivation for completing the assignment? Did you get the results you wanted? Compare this with your Christian journey, what is your motivation for obeying God?

school: motivation always to safeguard my final grade

Christian:

motivation: I say to: honor God (which I really do want to do) deep down doing it for personal desires & not the Lords desires (which I desperately want to become mine) also because I see the beauty of other peoples relationship w/ God & I want a beautiful relationship like theirs

Though now I try & clarify I want my own unique & intimate relationship w/ God & I really want it to be authentic....

Now that you've completed your self-reflection, seek God's forgiveness, repent and focus on being pure in your obedience. Thank God for His forgiveness and say a positive affirmation to yourself for the growth happening within you.

CHAPTER ONE

THE SYSTEM

DAY TWO

Focus Verse: *I run toward the goal, so that I can win the prize of being called to heaven. This is the prize that God offers because of what Christ Jesus has done. Philippians 3:14 CEV*

Devotional Question: In this chapter, we talked about focusing on your true assignment, do you have a clear understanding of your assignment? If so, what is it? Are you currently on the correct path to completing your assignment? If not, why? If you don't have a clear understanding of your true assignment or you are not making progress, write down the steps you will take with God to obtain the clarity you need to focus on your true assignment.

① Keep praying & strengthening
my prayer life
→ learning how to be clear
w/ my prayer as much as I
can & trusting the spirit to groan

② Keep working on my thesis & applying
to Ph.D. programs, Relay, & jobs

I'm not quite sure of my assignment Last thing God told me to do was pray and I honestly don't know any steps I could take...

Now that you've completed your self-reflection, seek God's forgiveness, repent and focus on being pure in your obedience. Thank God for His forgiveness and say a positive affirmation to yourself for the growth happening within you.

CHAPTER ONE

THE SYSTEM

DAY THREE

Focus Verse: *Now if you will obey me and keep my covenant, you will be my own special treasure from among all the peoples on earth; for all the earth belongs to me. Exodus 19:5 NLT*

Devotional Question: Since you understand your motivation for obeying God, what did you discover? Are you obeying Him because you desire something or just because He is God? What do you feel will happen if you don't obey God? Does your motivation align with having an authentic relationship with God? Please be authentic in your response.

I've discovered some motivations are because I desire something; the other is just because he's God & sacrificed his son. I want all of my motivations to be pure & glorify God. I got nervous a couple of weeks ago when I sinned my biggest fear was I'd never understand my purpose, I'd be punished, & the scariest being removed from his presence. It revealed I have some fundamentals I need to evaluate around God's nature. that however if my

ultimate goal: gaining spiritual
insight & growing in my knowledge of
God to serve him.
I desire authentic relationship
w/ God. I want to live for God.

Now that you've completed your self-reflection, seek God's forgiveness, repent and focus on being pure in your obedience. Thank God for His forgiveness and say a positive affirmation to yourself for the growth happening within you.

CHAPTER ONE

THE SYSTEM

DAY FOUR

Focus Verse: *They worshiped their idols, which led to their downfall. Psalm 106:36 NLT*

Devotional Question: In this chapter, we talked about idols. What idols you are playing host to you thought were a secret to God? How do you feel about your idols? What purpose do they serve in your life? Reflecting on your obedience to God, is your obedience motivated by the manifestation of your idols?

_____

_____

_____

_____

_____

_____

_____

_____

_____

_____

_____

_____

_____

_____

_____

_____

_____

_____

_____

_____

_____

_____

_____

_____

Now that you've completed your self-reflection, seek God's forgiveness, repent and focus on being pure in your obedience. Thank God for His forgiveness and say a positive affirmation to yourself for the growth happening within you.

CHAPTER ONE

THE SYSTEM

DAY FIVE

Focus Verse: *Nevertheless, each person should live as a believer in whatever situation the Lord has assigned to them, just as God has called them. This is the rule I lay down in all the churches. 1 Corinthians 7:17 NIV*

Devotional Question: Day Two of this devotional was focused on understanding your true assignment. If you know what your true assignment is, what are you doing to stay focused? If He hasn't revealed your assignment, what are you passionate about? What do you feel God is calling you to do? What breaks your heart? Understanding the things that break your heart may provide insight on your true assignment.

_____

_____

_____

_____

_____

_____

_____

_____

_____

_____

_____

_____

_____

_____

_____

_____

_____

_____

_____

_____

_____

Now that you've completed your self-reflection, seek God's forgiveness, repent and focus on being pure in your obedience. Thank God for His forgiveness and say a positive affirmation to yourself for the growth happening within you.

CHAPTER TWO

GAMBLING WITH GOD'S GRACE

DEVOTIONAL

CHAPTER TWO

GAMBLING WITH GOD'S GRACE

DAY SIX

Focus Verse: *I am sending you out like sheep among wolves. Therefore be as shrewd as snakes and as innocent as doves. Matthew 10:16 NIV*

Devotional Question: How do you feel when people only do something kind for you because they're expecting something in return? Did it make you feel used? Reflect on a time when this happened to you, what was your reaction?

_____

_____

_____

_____

_____

_____

_____

_____

_____

_____

_____

_____

_____

_____

_____

_____

_____

_____

_____

_____

_____

_____

Now that you've completed your self-reflection, seek God's forgiveness, repent and focus on being pure in your obedience. Thank God for His forgiveness and say a positive affirmation to yourself for the growth happening within you.

CHAPTER TWO

GAMBLING WITH GOD'S GRACE

DAY SEVEN

Focus Verse: *When the Lord Jesus had finished talking with them, he was taken up into heaven and sat down in the place of honor at God's right hand. Mark 16:19 NLT*

Devotional Question: In this Chapter, we discussed Jesus being a perfect example of God providing better winnings than what Jesus desired. How does Jesus' example assist in your thinking of God's winnings designed for you vs your desired winnings? Does this example help you trust Him and provide realignment of your motives?

_____

_____

_____

_____

_____

_____

_____

_____

_____

_____

_____

_____

_____

_____

_____

_____

_____

_____

_____

_____

_____

_____

Now that you've completed your self-reflection, seek God's forgiveness, repent and focus on being pure in your obedience. Thank God for His forgiveness and say a positive affirmation to yourself for the growth happening within you.

CHAPTER TWO

GAMBLING WITH GOD'S GRACE

DAY EIGHT

Focus Verse: *But he will pour out his anger and wrath on those who live for themselves, who refuse to obey the truth and instead live lives of wickedness. Romans 2:8 NLT*

Devotional Question: Do you have any examples where you gambled with God's grace? Did you receive a reward that was what you needed and not what you wanted? Reflect on this example and think on how this can serve as a reminder when your motives get off track.

_____

_____

_____

_____

_____

_____

_____

_____

_____

_____

_____

_____

_____

_____

_____

Now that you've completed your self-reflection, seek God's forgiveness, repent and focus on being pure in your obedience. Thank God for His forgiveness and say a positive affirmation to yourself for the growth happening within you.

CHAPTER TWO

GAMBLING WITH GOD'S GRACE

DAY NINE

Focus Verse: *Life will go well for those who freely lend and are honest in business. Psalm 112:5 CEV*

Devotional Question: Being rewarded without expectations, think about a time when this happened to you. How did you feel? Did you get a feeling of thankfulness and confirmation your work wasn't in vain? How would you feel if God rewarded you without your expectation? Think about how amazing it would be.

_____

_____

_____

_____

_____

_____

_____

_____

_____

_____

_____

_____

_____

_____

_____

_____

_____

_____

_____

_____

_____

_____

_____

Now that you've completed your self-reflection, seek God's forgiveness, repent and focus on being pure in your obedience. Thank God for His forgiveness and say a positive affirmation to yourself for the growth happening within you.

CHAPTER TWO

GAMBLING WITH GOD'S GRACE

DAY TEN

Focus Verse: *You're blessed when you get your inside world—your mind and heart—put right. Then you can see God in the outside world. Matthew 5:8 MSG*

Devotional Question: Sincerity, what does this word mean to you? What actions can you take to ensure you are sincere in your obedience to God?

_____

_____

_____

_____

_____

_____

_____

_____

_____

_____

_____

_____

_____

_____

_____

_____

_____

_____

_____

_____

_____

_____

Now that you've completed your self-reflection, seek God's forgiveness, repent and focus on being pure in your obedience. Thank God for His forgiveness and say a positive affirmation to yourself for the growth happening within you.

CHAPTER THREE

IT'S A SETUP

DEVOTIONAL

CHAPTER THREE

IT'S A SETUP

DAY ELEVEN

Focus Verse: *The one who does what is sinful is of the devil, because the devil has been sinning from the beginning. The reason the Son of God appeared was to destroy the devil's work. 1 John 3:8 NIV*

Devotional Question: The devil will use tricks to manipulate you to try to get an advantage over God. Think about a time when the devil has manipulated you. Did you fall victim to his tactics? Write your Adam & Eve story.

_____

_____

_____

_____

_____

_____

_____

_____

_____

_____

_____

_____

_____

_____

_____

_____

_____

_____

_____

_____

_____

_____

_____

_____

Now that you've completed your self-reflection, seek God's forgiveness, repent and focus on being pure in your obedience. Thank God for His forgiveness and say a positive affirmation to yourself for the growth happening within you.

CHAPTER THREE

IT'S A SETUP

DAY TWELVE

Focus Verse: *Each one should test their own actions. Then they can take pride in themselves alone, without comparing themselves to someone else, for each one should carry their own load. Galatians 6:4-5 NIV*

Devotional Question: Comparison, one of the commonly used tactics of the enemy. Reflect on the last time you fell prey to comparison and compared your situation to someone else's. Why did you feel the need to compare? What did you conclude from your comparison? What do you think was different about their situation compared to yours?

_____

_____

_____

_____

_____

_____

_____

_____

_____

_____

_____

_____

_____

_____

_____

_____

_____

_____

_____

_____

Now that you've completed your self-reflection, seek God's forgiveness, repent and focus on being pure in your obedience. Thank God for His forgiveness and say a positive affirmation to yourself for the growth happening within you.

CHAPTER THREE

IT'S A SETUP

DAY THIRTEEN

Focus Verse: *My son, pay attention to my wisdom; listen carefully to my wise counsel. Then you will show discernment, and your lips will express what you've learned. Proverbs 5:1-2 NLT*

Devotional Question: Distraction, the other tactic highlighted in this book. Think of a time where you were distracted by the enemy and you were heading down a path you thought was right only to learn you were headed in the opposite direction of God's plan for you. How did you feel? Did you get upset with God? Why? What were some of the questions you asked God?

_____

_____

_____

_____

_____

_____

_____

_____

_____

_____

_____

_____

_____

_____

_____

_____

_____

_____

_____

_____

_____

Now that you've completed your self-reflection, seek God's forgiveness, repent and focus on being pure in your obedience. Thank God for His forgiveness and say a positive affirmation to yourself for the growth happening within you.

CHAPTER THREE

IT'S A SETUP

DAY FOURTEEN

Focus Verse: *The Lord says: My thoughts and my ways are not like yours. Just as the heavens are higher than the earth, my thoughts and my ways are higher than yours. Isaiah 55:8-9 CEV*

Devotional Question: Continuing the topic from Day Thirteen, in your questioning of God, did God answer you? If so, did you conclude that you started falling short on your commitments to God? How did the revelation make you feel? If not, write a sincere prayer asking God to reveal to you answers to your questions.

_____

_____

_____

_____

_____

_____

_____

_____

_____

_____

_____

_____

_____

_____

_____

_____

_____

_____

_____

_____

_____

_____

_____

Now that you've completed your self-reflection, seek God's forgiveness, repent and focus on being pure in your obedience. Thank God for His forgiveness and say a positive affirmation to yourself for the growth happening within you.

CHAPTER THREE

IT'S A SETUP

DAY FIFTEEN

Focus Verse: *Look, I have given you authority over all the power of the enemy, and you can walk among snakes and scorpions and crush them. Nothing will injure you. Luke 10:19 NLT*

Devotional Question: This book highlighted two of the various tactics, distraction and comparison, the enemy can use to manipulate you from staying aligned to God's plan. Now, you should be more aware when you are all falling into the trap of the devil. What actions can you take to defend against the devil's tactics? How do you remind yourself to do this daily?

_____

_____

_____

_____

_____

_____

_____

_____

_____

_____

_____

_____

_____

_____

_____

_____

_____

_____

_____

Now that you've completed your self-reflection, seek God's forgiveness, repent and focus on being pure in your obedience. Thank God for His forgiveness and say a positive affirmation to yourself for the growth happening within you.

CHAPTER FOUR

YOUR HEART IDOLS

DEVOTIONAL

CHAPTER FOUR

YOUR HEART IDOLS

DAY SIXTEEN

Focus Verse: *The human heart is the most deceitful of all things, and desperately wicked. Who really knows how bad it is? Jeremiah 17:9 NLT*

Devotional Question: Our hearts can be deceitful. Recall a recent time when your heart deceived you, how bad was the deception? Was anyone else impacted? Were you able to recover? If so, how?

_____

_____

_____

_____

_____

_____

_____

_____

_____

_____

_____

_____

_____

_____

_____

_____

_____

_____

_____

_____

_____

Now that you've completed your self-reflection, seek God's forgiveness, repent and focus on being pure in your obedience. Thank God for His forgiveness and say a positive affirmation to yourself for the growth happening within you.

CHAPTER FOUR

YOUR HEART IDOLS

DAY SEVENTEEN

Focus Verse: *Those who work their land will have plenty to eat, but those who engage in empty pursuits have no sense. Proverbs 12:11 CEB*

Devotional Question: There are many things we are doing for God in hope He will bless us. In this chapter, they were called "it". What is your "it"? Why are you committed to this particular "it"?

_____

_____

_____

_____

_____

_____

_____

_____

_____

_____

_____

_____

_____

_____

_____

_____

_____

_____

_____

_____

_____

_____

_____

_____

_____

Now that you've completed your self-reflection, seek God's forgiveness, repent and focus on being pure in your obedience. Thank God for His forgiveness and say a positive affirmation to yourself for the growth happening within you.

CHAPTER FOUR

YOUR HEART IDOLS

DAY EIGHTEEN

Focus Verse: *Those who worship false gods turn their backs on all God's mercies. Jonah 2:8 NLT*

Devotional Question: Idols, if not identified could cause us to lose focus on God's purpose. Have your idols caused you to lose focus?

_____

_____

_____

_____

_____

_____

_____

_____

_____

_____

_____

_____

_____

_____

_____

_____

_____

_____

_____

_____

_____

_____

_____

Now that you've completed your self-reflection, seek God's forgiveness, repent and focus on being pure in your obedience. Thank God for His forgiveness and say a positive affirmation to yourself for the growth happening within you.

CHAPTER FOUR

YOUR HEART IDOLS

DAY NINETEEN

Focus Verse: *Whatever you do, do it from the heart for the Lord and not for people. You know that you will receive an inheritance as a reward. You serve the Lord Christ. Colossians 3:23-24 CEB*

Devotional Question: Are you cheating on God? List the areas in your life where you are not giving your all. What areas are you giving your all? What's the difference?

_____

_____

_____

_____

_____

_____

_____

_____

_____

_____

_____

_____

_____

_____

_____

_____

_____

_____

_____

_____

_____

_____

Now that you've completed your self-reflection, seek God's forgiveness, repent and focus on being pure in your obedience. Thank God for His forgiveness and say a positive affirmation to yourself for the growth happening within you.

CHAPTER FOUR

YOUR HEART IDOLS

DAY TWENTY

Focus Verse: *So humble yourselves before God. Resist the devil, and he will flee from you. Come close to God, and God will come close to you. Wash your hands, you sinners; purify your hearts, for your loyalty is divided between God and the world. James 4:7-8 NLT*

Devotional Question: Since you have identified the areas where you are not giving God your all, what steps can you take daily to ensure your heart and motives are pure? How will you implement the steps? When will you implement them? Challenge yourself to implement them sooner than later.

_____

_____

_____

_____

_____

_____

_____

_____

_____

_____

_____

_____

_____

_____

_____

_____

_____

_____

_____

_____

Now that you've completed your self-reflection, seek God's forgiveness, repent and focus on being pure in your obedience. Thank God for His forgiveness and say a positive affirmation to yourself for the growth happening within you.

CHAPTER FIVE

RAISING YOUR MATURITY IN CHRIST

DEVOTIONAL

CHAPTER FIVE

RAISING YOUR MATURITY IN CHRIST

DAY TWENTY-ONE

Focus Verse: *But God showed his great love for us by sending Christ to die for us while we were still sinners. Romans 5:8 NLT*

Devotional Question: Trusting God fully can be a hard task, but for us to ascend to greater levels with God we must trust Him confidently. In your authentic self, why is it so hard to fully trust God with all things, including our deepest desires?

_____

_____

_____

_____

_____

_____

_____

_____

_____

_____

_____

_____

_____

_____

_____

_____

_____

_____

_____

_____

_____

_____

Now that you've completed your self-reflection, seek God's forgiveness, repent and focus on being pure in your obedience. Thank God for His forgiveness and say a positive affirmation to yourself for the growth happening within you.

CHAPTER FIVE

RAISING YOUR MATURITY IN CHRIST

DAY TWENTY-TWO

Focus Verse: *Let them praise the Lord for his great love and for the wonderful things he has done for them. For he satisfies the thirsty and fills the hungry with good things. Psalm 107:8-9 NLT*

Devotional Question: A mindset of gratitude will help allow you to focus on the positive aspects in your life. What are you thankful for? What steps can you take to move to a constant attitude of thankfulness? How can you allow your gratitude to overshadow your desires?

_____

_____

_____

_____

_____

_____

_____

_____

_____

_____

_____

_____

_____

_____

_____

_____

_____

_____

_____

_____

_____

_____

_____

Now that you've completed your self-reflection, seek God's forgiveness, repent and focus on being pure in your obedience. Thank God for His forgiveness and say a positive affirmation to yourself for the growth happening within you.

CHAPTER FIVE

RAISING YOUR MATURITY IN CHRIST

DAY TWENTY-THREE

Focus Verse: *Think how much the Father loves us. He loves us so much that he lets us be called his children, as we truly are. But since the people of this world did not know who Christ is, they don't know who we are. 1 John 3:1 CEV*

Devotional Question: God's love is unconditional. What are some words you can use to describe God's love for you? How can you use those words to help provide you hope in relation to your desires? Write a prayer describing God's love.

_____

_____

_____

_____

_____

_____

_____

_____

_____

_____

_____

_____

_____

_____

_____

_____

_____

_____

_____

_____

_____

Now that you've completed your self-reflection, seek God's forgiveness, repent and focus on being pure in your obedience. Thank God for His forgiveness and say a positive affirmation to yourself for the growth happening within you.

CHAPTER FIVE

RAISING YOUR MATURITY IN CHRIST

DAY TWENTY-FOUR

Focus Verse: *God blesses those people who want to obey him more than to eat or drink. They will be given what they want! Matthew 5:6 CEV*

Devotional Question: Do you always have to be in control? Do you struggle with giving up control? Why do you like being in control? Can you think about a time when you gave up control of something to God? What was the outcome? What areas do you now need to give control over to God?

_____

_____

_____

_____

_____

_____

_____

_____

_____

_____

_____

_____

_____

_____

_____

_____

_____

_____

_____

_____

_____

_____

Now that you've completed your self-reflection, seek God's forgiveness, repent and focus on being pure in your obedience. Thank God for His forgiveness and say a positive affirmation to yourself for the growth happening within you.

CHAPTER FIVE

RAISING YOUR MATURITY IN CHRIST

DAY TWENTY-FIVE

Focus Verse: *Don't be like the people of this world, but let God change the way you think. Then you will know how to do everything that is good and pleasing to him. Romans 12:2 CEV*

Devotional Question: What steps will you take to increase your maturity in God?

_____

_____

_____

_____

_____

_____

_____

_____

_____

_____

_____

_____

_____

_____

_____

_____

_____

_____

_____

_____

_____

_____

_____

Now that you've completed your self-reflection, seek God's forgiveness, repent and focus on being pure in your obedience. Thank God for His forgiveness and say a positive affirmation to yourself for the growth happening within you.

CHAPTER SIX

SINCERELY OBEY GOD

DEVOTIONAL

CHAPTER SIX

SINCERELY OBEY GOD

DAY TWENTY-SIX

Focus Verse: *"...Blessed rather are those who hear the word of God and obey it."* Luke 11:28 NIV

Devotional Question: Sincere obedience and a God focused life work in concert with each other; together they will help minimize and/or eliminate the pressures of life. What mindset changes are you going to make to ensure you're operating in sincere obedience? How do you maintain a God focused life?

_____

_____

_____

_____

_____

_____

_____

_____

_____

_____

_____

_____

_____

_____

_____

_____

_____

_____

_____

_____

_____

_____

Now that you've completed your self-reflection, seek God's forgiveness, repent and focus on being pure in your obedience. Thank God for His forgiveness and say a positive affirmation to yourself for the growth happening within you.

CHAPTER SIX

SINCERELY OBEY GOD

DAY TWENTY-SEVEN

Focus Verse: *If you keep yourself pure, you will be a special utensil for honorable use. Your life will be clean, and you will be ready for the Master to use you for every good work. 2 Timothy 2:21 NLT*

Devotional Question: Pureness in action should be the goal. What impurities will you ask God to remove? What commitment will you make to God to ensure you are always operating in pureness?

_____

_____

_____

_____

_____

_____

_____

_____

_____

_____

_____

_____

_____

_____

_____

_____

_____

_____

_____

_____

_____

_____

_____

_____

Now that you've completed your self-reflection, seek God's forgiveness, repent and focus on being pure in your obedience. Thank God for His forgiveness and say a positive affirmation to yourself for the growth happening within you.

CHAPTER SIX

SINCERELY OBEY GOD

DAY TWENTY-EIGHT

Focus Verse: *Christ has set us free! This means we are really free. Now hold on to your freedom and don't ever become slaves of the Law again. Galatians 5:1 CEV*

Devotional Question: A life of freedom, how wonderful does that sound? What does a life of freedom look like to you? How peaceful will your life be? What steps are you going to take to help you move towards a life of freedom?

_____

_____

_____

_____

_____

_____

_____

_____

_____

_____

_____

_____

_____

_____

_____

_____

_____

_____

_____

_____

_____

_____

Now that you've completed your self-reflection, seek God's forgiveness, repent and focus on being pure in your obedience. Thank God for His forgiveness and say a positive affirmation to yourself for the growth happening within you.

CHAPTER SIX

SINCERELY OBEY GOD

DAY TWENTY-NINE

Focus Verse: *And you must love the Lord your God with all your heart, all your soul, all your mind, and all your strength. The second is equally important: 'Love your neighbor as yourself. No other commandment is greater than these." Mark 12:30-31 NLT*

Devotional Question: Love should be the guide for everything we do for God and others. Moving forward, how will you let love be the guidepost for everything you do?

_____

_____

_____

_____

_____

_____

_____

_____

_____

_____

_____

_____

_____

_____

_____

_____

_____

_____

_____

_____

_____

_____

_____

Now that you've completed your self-reflection, seek God's forgiveness, repent and focus on being pure in your obedience. Thank God for His forgiveness and say a positive affirmation to yourself for the growth happening within you.

CHAPTER SIX

SINCERELY OBEY GOD

DAY THIRTY

Focus Verse: *Be careful to obey all these commands I am giving you. Show love to the Lord your God by walking in his ways and holding tightly to him. Deuteronomy 11:22 NLT*

Devotional Question: What are the major takeaways from this book? How are you going to apply them to help your life?

_____

_____

_____

_____

_____

_____

_____

_____

_____

_____

_____

_____

_____

_____

_____

_____

_____

_____

_____

_____

_____

_____

_____

_____

Now that you've completed your self-reflection, seek God's forgiveness, repent and focus on being pure in your obedience. Thank God for His forgiveness and say a positive affirmation to yourself for the growth happening within you.

FINAL WORD

I pray this book has been a blessing to you and you decide to be pure in your relationship with the Father. Nothing feels better than being in an authentic relationship. Ever since I've had this revelation, it has been a sounding board to my actions for God. There are times I might use it in other relationships if it warrants it. Make a resolve to obey God with a pure heart.

CLOSING PRAYER

God, how excellent is your name. Lord, we are sorry for not having a pure heart while being obedient to you. Forgive us for our disobedience and ignorance. Lord, create in us a clean heart so that our motives are pure. Your word says that you will reward those who sincerely seek you. Lord, we believe it, so we are here declaring sincerity in pursuing and we will leave the rewards up to you. Lord, bless our lives. We love you God and we ask all these things in your son Jesus' name.

Amen.

ABOUT THE AUTHOR

 **LaNessa Jackson's** mission in life is to help others be successful in reaching their goals. Personal growth is one of her main focus. She's a Computer Scientist by trade and currently works for a Fortune 100 company solving technical business problems. LaNessa has a degree in Computer Science from Grambling State University and an MBA from Kaplan University. She holds Project Management Professional (PMP) and 6 Sigma Black Belt certificates. LaNessa's passion for helping people motivated her to embark on this journey. She loves God and has a desire to help people grow closer in their relationship. LaNessa is the owner of *A Dream Realized*, a consulting company founded to provide personal finance and business coaching. In her spare time, LaNessa loves to workout, read and spend time with family and friends.

Thank you for taking the time to read this book. I pray this book was a blessing and provided you with practical guidance on how you can improve your relationship with God.

Made in the USA
Lexington, KY
08 July 2019